Bread Machine Recipes

for Beginners

The Most Funny Cooking Guide Adaptable To

Any Bread Maker. Bring the Authentic Taste of

Homemade Bread to Your Table

Layla Baker

TABLE OF CONTENTS

INTRODUCTION

Bread making machine, otherwise known as a bread maker, is a home-based appliance that transforms uncooked ingredients into bread. It is made up of a saucepan for bread (or "tin"), with one or more built-in paddles at the bottom, present in the center of a small special-purpose oven. This little oven is usually operated via a control panel via a simple in-built computer utilizing the input settings. Some bread machines have diverse cycles for various forms of dough — together with white bread, whole grain, European-style (occasionally called "French"), and dough-only (for pizza dough and formed loaves baked in a traditional oven). Many also have a timer to enable the bread machine to work without the operator's attendance, and some high-end models allow the user to program a customized period.

To bake bread, ingredients are measured in a specified order into the bread pan (usually first liquids, with solid ingredients layered on top), and then the pan is put in the bread maker. The order of ingredients is important because contact with water triggers the instant yeast used in bread makers, so the yeast and water have to be kept separate until the program starts.

It takes the machine several hours to make a bread loaf. The products are rested first and brought to an optimal temperature. Stir with a paddle, and the ingredients are then shaped into flour. Use optimal temperature regulation, and the dough is then confirmed and then cooked.

When the bread has been baked, the bread maker removes the pan. Then leaving a slight indentation from the rod to which the paddle is connected. The finished loaf's shape is often regarded as unique. Many initial bread machines manufacture a vertically slanted towards, square, or cylindrical loaf that is significantly dissimilar from commercial bread; however, more recent units typically have a more conventional horizontal pan. Some bread machines use two paddles to form two lb. loaf in regular rectangle shape.

Bread machine recipes are often much smaller than regular bread recipes. Sometimes standardized based on the bread machine's capacity, the most popular in the US market is 1.5 lb. /700 g units. Most recipes are written for that capacity; however, two lb. /900 g units are not uncommon. There are prepared bread mixes, specially made for bread makers, containing pre-measured ingredients and flour and yeast, flavorings, and sometimes dough conditioners.

Bread makers are also fitted with a timer for testing when bread-making starts. For example, this allows them to be loaded at night but only begin baking in the morning to produce freshly baked bread for breakfast. They may also be set only for making dough, for example, for making pizza. Apart from bread, some can also be set to make other things like jam, pasta dough, and Japanese rice cake. Some of the new developments in the facility of the machine include automatically adding nut. It also contains fruit from a tray during the kneading process. Bread makers typically take between three and four hours to bake a loaf. However, recent "quick bake" modes have become standard additions, many of which can produce a loaf in less than an hour.

DOUGH RECIPES

1. Cheddar Biscuits

Preparation Time: 10 minutes

Cooking Time: 25 minutes

Servings: 12

Ingredients:

- 3 eggs

- ¼ cup unsalted butter, melted

- 1 ¼ cups, coconut milk

- ¼ tsp. salt

- ¼ tsp. baking soda

- ¼ tsp. garlic powder

- ½ cup finely shredded sharp cheddar cheese

- 1 Tbsp. fresh herb

- 2/3 cup coconut flour

Directions:

1 Preheat the bread machine to 350F. Grease a baking sheet.

2 Mix together the butter, eggs, milk, salt, baking soda, garlic powder, cheese, and herbs until well blended.

3   Add the coconut flour to the batter and mix until well blended. Let the batter sit and then mix again.

4   Spoon about 2 tbsp. batter for each biscuit onto the greased baking sheet.

5   Bake for 25 minutes.

6   Serve warm.

Nutrition: Calories: 125 Fat: 7g Carb: 10g Protein: 5g

2. Savory Waffles

Preparation Time: 10 minutes

Cooking Time: 20 minutes

Servings: 4

Ingredients:

- 3 eggs
- 1 tsp. olive oil
- ½ cup sliced scallions
- ¾ cup grated pepper Jack cheese
- ¼ tsp. baking soda
- 1 Pinch salt
- 2 Tbsp. coconut flour

Directions:

1 Preheat the waffle iron to medium heat.

2 Mix all the ingredients using a bowl. Let the batter sit and mix once more.

3 Scoop ½ cup to 1-cup batter (depending on the size of the waffle iron) and pour onto the iron. Cook according to the manufacturer's directions.

4 Pour mixture into your bread machine pan.

5 Serve warm.

Nutrition: Calories: 183 Fat: 13g Carb: 4g Protein: 12g

3. Chocolate Chip Scones

Preparation Time: 10 minutes

Cooking Time: 10 minutes

Servings: 8

Ingredients:

- 2 cups almond flour
- 1 tsp. baking soda
- ¼ tsp. sea salt
- 1 egg
- 1 Tbsp. low-carb sweetener
- 3 Tbsp. milk, cream or yogurt
- ½ cup sugar-free chocolate chips

Directions:

1. Preheat the bread machine to 350F.
2. Using a bowl, add almond flour, baking soda, and salt and blend.
3. Then add the egg, sweetener, milk, and chocolate chips. Blend well.
4. Tap the dough into a ball and place it on parchment paper.
5. Roll the dough with a rolling pin into a large circle. Slice it into 8 triangular pieces.

6   Place the scones and parchment paper on a baking sheet and separate the scones about 1 inch or so apart.

7   For 7 to 10 minutes, bake until lightly browned.

8   Cool and serve.

Nutrition: Calories: 213 Fat: 18g Carb: 10g Protein: 8g

4. Snickerdoodles

Preparation Time: 10 minutes

Cooking Time: 10 minutes

Servings: 20

Ingredients:

- 3 cups almond flour
- Tbsp. coconut flour
- ¼ tsp. baking soda
- ¼ tsp. salt
- 1 Tbsp. unsalted butter, melted
- 1/3 cup low-carb sweetener
- ¼ cup coconut milk
- 1 Tbsp. vanilla extract
- 3 Tbsp. ground cinnamon
- 2 Tbsp. low-carb granulated sweetener

Directions:

1 Preheat the bread machine to 350F.

2 Whisk the almond flour, coconut flour, salt, and baking soda together using a bowl.

3 In another bowl, cream the butter, sweetener, milk, and vanilla.

4   Put the flour mixture to the butter mixture and blend well.

5   Line baking sheets with parchment paper.

6   Blend the ground cinnamon and low-carb granulated sweetener together in a bowl. With your hands, roll a tbsp. of dough into a ball.

7   Reel the dough ball in the cinnamon mixture to fully coat.

8   Put the dough balls on the cookie sheet, spread about an inch apart, and flatten with the underside of a jar.

9   Bake for 8 to 10 minutes.

10 Cool and serve.

Nutrition: Calories: 86 Fat: 7g Carb: 3g Protein: 3g

5. No Corn Cornbread

Preparation Time: 10 minutes

Cooking Time: 20 minutes

Servings: 8

Ingredients:

- ½ cup almond flour
- ¼ cup coconut flour
- ¼ tsp. salt
- ¼ tsp. baking soda
- 2 eggs
- ¼ cup unsalted butter
- 1Tbsp. low-carb sweetener

- ½ cup coconut milk

Directions:

1   Preheat the bread machine to 325F. Line a baking pan.

2   Combine dry ingredients in a bowl.

3   Put all the dry ingredients to the wet ones and blend well.

4   Dispense the batter into the baking pan and bake for 20 minutes.

5   Cool, slice, and serve.

Nutrition: Calories: 65 Fat: 6g Carb: 2g Protein: 2g

6. Garlic Cheese Bread Loaf

Preparation Time: 10 minutes

Cooking Time: 45 minutes

Servings: 10

Ingredients:

- 1 Tbsp. parsley, chopped
- ½ cup butter, unsalted and softened
- 1 Tbsp. garlic powder
- 3 large eggs
- ½ tsp. oregano seasoning
- 1 tsp. baking powder
- 3 cups almond flour
- ½ tsp. xanthan gum
- 1 cup cheddar cheese, shredded
- ½ tsp. salt

Directions:

1. Preheat the bread machine to 355F.
2. Line a baking pan with parchment paper.
3. In a food blender, pulse the eggs until smooth. Then combine the butter and pulse for 1 minute more.

4   Blend the almond flour and baking powder for 90 seconds or until it thickens.

5   Finally, combine the garlic, oregano, parsley, and cheese until mixed.

6   Pour into the prepared and bake in the bread machine for 45 minutes.

7   Cool, slice, and serve.

Nutrition: Calories: 299 Fat: 27g Carb: 4g Protein: 11g

7. Iranian Flat Bread (Sangak)

Preparation Time: 3 hours

Cooking Time: 15 minutes

Servings: 6

Ingredients:

- 3 cups almond flour
- ½ cups warm water
- 1 Tbsp. instant yeast
- 1 tsp. sesame seeds
- Salt to taste

Directions:

1   Add 1 tbsp. yeast to ½ cup warm water using a bowl and allow to stand for 5 minutes.

2   Add salt add 1 cup of water. Let stand for 10 minutes longer.

3   Put one cup of flour at a time and then add the remaining water.

4   Knead the dough and then shape it into a ball and let stand for 3 hours covered.

5   Preheat the bread machine to 480F.

6   By means of a rolling pin, roll out the dough, and divide into 6 balls.

7   Roll each ball into ½ inch thick rounds.

8   Place a parchment paper on the baking sheet and place the rolled rounds on it.

9   With a finger, make a small hole in the middle and add 2 tsp sesame seeds in each hole.

10 Bake for 3 to 4 minutes, then flip over and bake for 2 minutes more.

11 Serve.

Nutrition: Calories: 26 Fat: 1g Carb: 3.5g Protein: 0.7g

8. Chocolate Zucchini Bread

Preparation Time: 10 minutes

Cooking Time: 20 minutes

Servings: 10

Ingredients:

- 2 cups grated zucchini, excess moisture removed

- 3 eggs

- 1 Tbsp. olive oil

- 1/3 cup low-carb sweetener

- 1 tsp. vanilla extract

- 1/3 cup coconut flour

- ¼ cup unsweetened cocoa powder

- ½ tsp. baking soda

- ½ tsp. salt

- 1/3 cup sugar-free chocolate chips

Directions:

1 Preheat the bread machine to 350F.

2 Grease the baking pan and line the entire pan with parchment paper.

3   In a food processor, blend the eggs, zucchini, oil, sweetener, and vanilla.

4   Add the flour, cocoa, baking soda, and salt to the zucchini mixture and stir until mixed. For a few seconds, let the batter sit.

5   Mix in the chocolate chips, then dispense the batter into the prepared pan.

6   Bake for 45 to 50 minutes.

7   Cool, slice, and serve.

Nutrition: Calories: 149 Fat: 8g Carb: 7g Protein: 3g

9. Cauliflower Breadsticks

Preparation Time: 10 minutes

Cooking Time: 35 minutes

Servings: 8

Ingredients:

- 3 cups riced cauliflower

- 1 cup mozzarella, shredded

- 1 tsp. Italian seasoning

- 2 eggs

- ½ tsp. ground pepper

- 1 tsp. salt

- ½ tsp. granulated garlic

- ¼ cup Parmesan cheese as a topping

Directions:

1 Preheat the bread machine to 350F. Grease a baking sheet.

2 Beat the eggs until mixed well.

3 Combine riced cauliflower, mozzarella cheese, Italian seasoning, pepper, garlic, and salt and blend on low speed in a food processor. Combine with eggs.

4   Pour the dough into the prepared cookie sheet and pat the dough down to ¼ thick across the pan.

5   Bake for 30 minutes and dust the breadsticks with the parmesan cheese.

6   Put the breadsticks on the broil setting for 2 to 3 minutes, so the cheese melts.

7   Slice and serve.

Nutrition: Calories: 165 Fat: 10g Carb: 5g Protein: 13g

10.Cheddar Crackers

Preparation Time: 10 minutes

Cooking Time: 55 minutes

Servings: 8

Ingredients:

- 1 Tbsp. unsalted butter, softened slightly

- 1 egg white

- ¼ tsp. salt

- 1 cup plus 2 Tbsp. almond flour

- 1 tsp. minced fresh thyme

- 1 cup shredded sharp white cheddar cheese

Directions:

1 Preheat the bread machine to 300F.

2 Using a bowl, beat together the butter, egg white, and salt.

3 Stir in the almond flour and thyme and then the cheddar until mixed.

4 Move the dough out between two pieces of parchment paper to a rectangle.

5 Peel off the top parchment paper and place the dough with the bottom parchment paper on a sheet pan.

6   Cut the dough into crackers with a pizza cutter.

7   Bake until golden, about 45 to 55 minutes, rotating the tray once halfway through.

8   Cool and serve.

Nutrition: Calories: 200 Fat: 18g Carb: 4g Protein: 7g

11. Sesame Almond Crackers

Preparation Time: 10 minutes

Cooking Time: 24 minutes

Servings: 8

Ingredients:

- 1 Tbsp. unsalted butter, softened slightly

- 2 egg whites

- ½ tsp. salt

- ¼ tsp. black pepper

- ¼ cups almond flour

- 3 Tbsp. sesame seeds

Directions:

1 Preheat the bread machine to 350F.

2 Using a bowl, beat the egg whites, butter, salt, and black pepper.

3 Stir in the almond flour and sesame seeds.

4 Move the dough out between two pieces of parchment paper to a rectangle.

5 Peel off the top parchment paper and place the dough on a sheet pan.

6 Cut the dough into crackers with a pizza cutter.

7 Bake for 18 to 24 minutes, or until golden, rotating the tray halfway through.

8 Serve.

Nutrition: Calories: 299 Fat: 28g Carb: 4g Protein: 8g

12.No-Yeast Sourdough Starter

Preparation Time: 10 minutes

Cooking Time: 0 minutes

Servings: 64

Ingredients:

- 3 cups all-purpose flour
- 3 cups chlorine-free bottled water at room temperature

Directions:

1   Stir together the flour and water in a large glass bowl with a wooden spoon.

2   With a plastic wrap, cover the bowl and place it in a warm area for 3 to 4 days, stirring at least twice a day, or until bubbly.

3   Put ingredients in the bread maker.

4   Store the starter in the refrigerator in a covered glass jar and stir it before using.

5   Replenish your starter by adding back the same amount you removed, in equal parts flour and water.

Nutrition: Calories: 14 Fat: 0g Carbohydrates: 3g Fiber: 0g Protein: 0g

13.Pizza Dough

Preparation Time: 10 minutes

Cooking Time: 1 hour 30 minutes

Servings: 2

Ingredients:

- 1 cup of warm water
- ¾ teaspoon salt
- 2 tablespoons olive oil
- 2 ½ cups flour
- 2 teaspoons sugar
- 2 teaspoons yeast

Directions:

1. Put ingredients in the bread maker.
2. Enable the Dough program and start the cycle.
3. Put the finished dough in a greased form or pan and distribute it. Allow standing for 10 minutes.
4. Preheat the bread machine to 400°F. On top of the dough, place the pizza sauce and the filling. Top with grated cheese.
5. For 15 to 20 minutes, bake till the edge is browned.

Nutrition: Calories 716; Total Fat 15.7g; Saturated Fat 2.3g; Cholesterol 0mg; Sodium 881g; Total Carbohydrate 124.8g; Dietary Fiber 5.1g; Total Sugars 4.4 g; Protein 17.7g

14. Pizza Basis

Preparation Time: 10 minutes

Cooking Time: 1 hour 20 minutes

Servings: 2

Ingredients:

- 1 ¼ cups warm water
- 2 cups flour
- 1 cup Semolina flour
- ½ teaspoon sugar
- 1 teaspoon salt
- 1 teaspoon olive oil
- 2 teaspoons yeast

Directions:

1. Place all the ingredients in the bread maker's bucket in the order recommended by the manufacturer. Select the Dough program.

2. After the dough has risen, use it as the base for the pizza.

Nutrition: Calories 718; Total Fat 4.4g; Saturated Fat 0.6g; Cholesterol 0mg; Sodium 1173g; Total Carbohydrate 145.6g; Dietary Fiber 5.9g; Total Sugars 1.5 g; Protein 20.9g

15.Cinnamon Raisin Buns

Preparation Time: 10 minutes

Cooking Time: 45 minutes

Servings: 12

Ingredients:

For dough

- ½ cup milk
- ½ cup of water
- 2 tablespoons butter
- ¾ teaspoon salt
- 3 cups flour
- 2 ¼ teaspoon yeast
- 3 tablespoons sugar
- 1 egg

For filling

- 3 tablespoons butter, melted
- ¾ teaspoon ground cinnamon
- 1/3 cup sugar
- 1/3 cup raisins
- 1/3 cup chopped walnuts

For glaze

- 1 cup powdered sugar
- 1 ½ tablespoon melted butter
- ¼ teaspoon vanilla
- 1 ½ tablespoons milk

Directions:

1. In a saucepan, heat ½ cup of milk, water, and 2 tablespoons of butter until they become hot.

2. Put the milk mixture, salt, flour, yeast, sugar, and eggs in the bread maker's bucket in the order recommended by the manufacturer. Select the Dough program. Click Start.

3. When through with the cycle, take out the dough from the bread maker. On a flour-covered surface, roll the dough into a large rectangle. Lubricate with softened butter.

4. Mix the cinnamon and sugar. Sprinkle the rectangle with the mixture. Generously sprinkle with raisins and/or chopped nuts.

5. Roll the dough into a roll, starting from the long side. Cut into 12 pieces. Put the buns slit-side down on a greased baking tray (25x35cm).

6. Cover and put in the heat until the dough almost doubles, about 30 minutes.

7. Preheat the bread machine to 375 degrees F. Mix the powdered sugar, 1 1/2 tablespoon melted butter, vanilla, and 1 ½ tablespoon milk to get a thick frosting; set it aside.

8. Bake the buns in a preheated bread machine for 20 - 25 minutes until browned. Remove and allow to cool down for 10 minutes. Frost the cooled buns with icing.

Nutrition: Calories 308; Total Fat 9.2g; Saturated Fat 4.3g; Cholesterol 31mg; Sodium 202g; Total Carbohydrate 53.2g; Dietary Fiber 1.5g; Total Sugars 27.9 g; Protein 5.2g

16.Italian Pie Calzone

Preparation Time: 5 minutes

Cooking Time: 1 hour 5 minutes

Servings: 12

Ingredients:

- 1 ¼ cups water

- 1 teaspoon salt

- 3 cups flour

- 1 teaspoon milk powder

- 1 ½ tablespoons sugar

- 2 teaspoons yeast

- ¾ cup tomato sauce for pizza

- 1 cup pepperoni sausage, finely chopped
- 1 ¼ cups grated mozzarella
- 2 tablespoons butter, melted

Directions:

1. Put water, salt, bread baking flour, soluble milk, sugar, and yeast in the bread maker's bucket in the order recommended by the manufacturer. Select the Dough setting.

2. After the end of the cycle, roll the dough on a lightly floured surface; form a rectangle measuring 45 x 25 cm. Transfer to a lightly oiled baking tray.

3. In a small bowl, combine the chopped pepperoni and mozzarella. Spoon the pizza sauce in a strip along the center of the dough. Add the filling of sausage and cheese.

4. Make diagonal incisions at a distance of 1 ½ cm from each other at the sides, receding 1 ½ cm from the filling.

5. Cross the strips on top of the filling, moistening it with the water. Lubricate with melted butter.

6. For 35 to 45 minutes bake at 360 degrees F.

Nutrition: Calories 247; Total Fat 9.2g; Saturated Fat 3.9g; Cholesterol 22mg; Sodium 590g; Total Carbohydrate 32g; Dietary Fiber 1.5g; Total Sugars 2.8 g; Protein 8.6g

17.French Baguettes

Preparation Time: 20 minutes

Cooking Time: 2 hours 30 minutes

Servings: 6

Ingredients:

- 1½ cups water

- 1½ teaspoons sugar

- 1½ teaspoons salt

- 3½ cups flour

- 1½ teaspoons yeast

- a mixture of different seeds (pumpkin, sunflower, black and white sesame)

Directions:

1. To prepare the dough for French baguettes in the bread maker, place all the ingredients in the bread maker's container in order: water, salt, and sugar, flour, yeast. Select the Yeast Dough program.

2. After 1½ hour, the dough for baguettes is ready.

3. Heat the bread machine to 440°F. Divide the dough into 2 parts. Lubricate the pan with oil. From the dough, form two French baguettes. Put on a baking pan and let it come for 10 minutes.

4. Then with a sharp knife, make shallow incisions on the surface of the baguettes. Sprinkle with water and sprinkle with a mixture of seeds. Leave it for another 10 minutes.

5. After the bread machine is warmed, put the pan with French baguettes in the bread machine for 5-7 minutes, then lower the heat to 360°F and bake for another 20-30 minutes until ready.

6. Transfer baguettes to a grate and cool.

7. Your crispy, delicious, fragrant French baguettes are ready… Bon appétit!

Nutrition: Calories 272; Total Fat 0.8g; Saturated Fat 0.1g; Cholesterol 0mg; Sodium 585g; Total Carbohydrate 57g; Dietary Fiber 2.2g; Total Sugars 1.2g; Protein 7.9g

BUNS & BREAD

18.Buns with Cottage Cheese

Preparation Time: 10 minutes

Cooking Time: 15 minutes

Servings: 8

Ingredients:

- 2 eggs

- 2 oz. Almond flour

- 1 oz. Erythritol

- 1/8 tsp. Stevia

- cinnamon and vanilla extract to taste

Filling:

- ½ oz. Cottage cheese

- 1 egg

- cinnamon and vanilla extract to taste

Directions:

1 Prepare the filling by mixing its ingredients in a bowl.

2 Combine eggs with almond flour, blend until smooth. Add erythritol, stevia, and flavors to taste.

3   Spoon 1 tbsp. Dough into silicone cups. Spoon about 1 tsp.

4   Position all ingredients in your bread machine pan in the order listed above.

5   Close the lid of your bread machine, select DOUGH cycle, and press START.

6   Filling on top, and bake at 365f for 15 minutes.

Nutrition: Calories: 77 Fat: 5.2g Carb: 6.7g Protein: 5.8g

19.Keto German Franks Bun

Preparation Time: 2 hours

Cooking Time: 9 minutes

Servings: 10

Ingredients:

- 1 ¼ cup almond milk, unsweetened, warmed

- ¼ cup sugar, granulated

- 1 small egg

- 2 tbsps. butter

- ¾ tsp. salt

- ¾ cups almond flour

- 1 ¼ tsps. active dry yeast

Directions:

1   Position all ingredients in your bread machine pan in the order listed above.

2   Close the lid of your bread machine, select DOUGH cycle, and press START.

3   Once the cycle is finished, transfer the dough to a floured surface. Cut the dough into 10 slices long.

4   Flatten the dough into 5 x 4 inches. Then firmly roll the dough to form a cylindrical shape size of 5 x 1 inch. Cover and let it rise for an hour or until the dough size doubles.

5   Preheat the bread machine to 350 degrees Fahrenheit. Arrange the dough on a greased baking sheet.

6   Place the baking sheet in the bread machine and bake for 9 minutes or until golden brown.

7   Cool and then serve with your favorite franks.

Nutrition: Calories: 16 Calories from fat: 87 Total Fat: 8 g Total Carbohydrates: 3 g Net Carbohydrates: 3 g

Protein: 6 g

20. Keto Beer Bread

Preparation Time: 10 minutes

Cooking Time: 0 minutes

Servings: 10

Ingredients:

- 1 oz. beer at room temperature
- 1 oz. American cheese, shredded
- 3 oz. Monterey Jack cheese, shredded
- 1 tbsp. sugar
- 1 ½ tsp. salt
- 1 tbsp. butter
- 3 cups almond flour
- 2 tsp. active dry yeast

Directions:

1. Using a microwave, combine beer and American cheese and warm for 20 seconds.

2. Transfer the beer mixture into the bread machine pan and add all the other ingredients as listed above.

3. Close the bread machine lid and select WHITE BREAD setting (or BASIC setting and press the START button.

4. When the cycle ends, cool the bread on a cooling rack.

5. Slice and then serve with a bowl of chili or beef stew.

Nutrition: Calories: 118 Calories from fat: 9 Total Fat: 9 Total Carbohydrates: 3 g Net Carbohydrates: 3 g

Protein: 6 g

21.Keto Monterey Jack Jalapeno Bread

Preparation Time: 15 minutes

Cooking Time: 0 minutes

Servings: 12

Ingredients:

- 1 cup water

- 2 tbsps. non-fat milk

- 1 ½ tbsps. sugar

- 1 ½ tsp. salt

- 1 ½ tbsps. butter, cubed

- ¼ cup Monterey Jack cheese, shredded

- 1 small jalapeno pepper

- 3 cups almond flour

- 1 tsp. active dry yeast

Directions:

1. Get rid of the seeds and stem of the jalapeno and mince finely.

2. Add the ingredients into the bread machine pan as listed above.

3. Close the lid and select BASIC cycle and light or medium CRUST COLOR, then press START.

4. Once the cycle ends, transfer the loaf to a cooling rack before slicing.

5. Serve as a side dish for salad or your favorite main course.

Nutrition: Calories: 47 Calories from fat: 27 Total Fat: 3 g Total Carbohydrates: 3 g Net Carbohydrates: 2 g

Protein: 2 g

22.   Keto Rye Sandwich Bread

Preparation Time: 10 minutes

Cooking Time: 3 hours

Servings: 12

Ingredients:

- ¼ cups warm water

- 1 tbsps. melted butter, unsalted

- 2 tsps. white sugar

- 1 ½ tsp. salt

- 1 tbsp. baking powder

- ¼ tsp. ground ginger

- ¼ cup granulated swerve

- 2 cups vital wheat gluten

- 3 cups super fine almond flour

- ¼ cup dark rye flour

- 1 tsps. Active dry yeast

- 1 tbsp. caraway seeds

Directions:

1   Position all ingredients in the bread machine bucket and close the
    lid.

2   Select the WHOLE WHEAT cycle in your bread machine setting and choose the light color on CRUST COLOR. Press START.

3   When the cycle ends, remove the pan from the bread machine and transfer the loaf to a cooling rack.

4   Slice and make a pastrami or Rueben sandwich to serve.

Nutrition: Calories: 275 Calories from fat: 144 Total Fat: 16 g Total Carbohydrates: 12 Net Carbohydrates: 8 g Protein: 22 g

23.   Keto Orange Cranberry Bread

Preparation Time: 10 minutes

Cooking Time: 0 minutes

Servings: 10

Ingredients:

- ¼ cup almond flour

- 1 tbsp. baking powder

- ¼ tsp. kosher salt

- 2 large eggs

- 1 ½ cup buttermilk

- 1 tbsp. canola oil

- 1 ½ cup brown sugar

- ½ tbsp. vanilla

- ½ tsp. nutmeg

- ¾ tsp. orange zest

- 2 tbsp. orange juice, fresh

- 1 cup fresh cranberries, chopped

Directions:

1. Position all the ingredients in your bread machine bucket except for the cranberries.

2. Close the bread machine before selecting the QUICK BREAD setting on your bread machine and then press START.

3. Wait for the ping or the fruit and nut signal to open the lid and add the chopped cranberries. Cover the lid again and press START to continue.

4. When the cycle finishes, transfer the loaf to a wire rack and let it cool.

5. Slice and serve with your favorite salad.

Nutrition: Calories: 141 Calories from fat: 110 Total Fat: 12 g Total Carbohydrates: 5 g Net Carbohydrates: 4 g Protein: 4 g

24.   Swiss Whole Meal Cheese Bread

Preparation Time: 3 hours

Cooking Time: 0 minutes

Servings: 8

Ingredients:

- ¾ cup warm water
- 1 tablespoon sugar
- 1 teaspoon salt
- 3 tablespoons green cheese
- 1 cup flour
- 9/10 cup flour whole-grain, finely ground
- 1 teaspoon yeast
- 1 teaspoon paprika

Directions:

1   Ingredients are listed in the order in which they are placed in the bread machine.

2   Add paprika at the signal.

3   The bread is gray, with a porous pulp. And it does not become stale for a long time. It has a unique flavor, with very interesting cheese notes.

Nutrition: Carbohydrates 5 g Fats 1 g Protein 4.1 g Calories 118

25.   Mustard Beer Bread

Preparation Time: 3 hours

Cooking Time: 0 minutes

Servings: 8

Ingredients:

- 1 ¼ cups dark beer

- 1/3 cups flour

- ¾ cup whole meal flour

- 1 tablespoon olive oil

- 3 teaspoons mustard seeds

- 1 ½ teaspoons dry yeast

- 1 teaspoon salt

- 2 teaspoons brown sugar

Directions:

1   Open a beer bottle and let it stand for 30 minutes to get out the gas.

2   In a bread maker's bucket, add the beer, mustard seeds, butter, sifted flour, and whole meal flour.

3   From different angles in the bucket, put salt and sugar. In the center of the flour, make a groove and fill it with the mustard seeds.

4   Start the baking program.

Nutrition: Carbohydrates 4.2 g Fats 1 g Protein 4.1 g Calories 118

26. Keto Flaxseed Honey Bread

Preparation Time: 10 minutes

Cooking Time: 20 minutes

Servings: 18 slices

Ingredients:

- 1 cup warm water
- 2 small eggs, lightly beaten
- ½ cup oat fiber
- 2/3 cup flaxseed meal
- 1.25 cup vital wheat gluten
- 1 tsp. salt
- 1 tbsp. swerve powdered sweetener
- 1 tsp. honey
- ½ tsp. xanthan gum
- 2 tbsps. Butter, unsalted
- 1 tbsp. dry active yeast

Directions:

1   Pour the water into the bread bucket.

2   Add the eggs, honey, erythritol, salt, oat fiber, flaxseed meal, wheat gluten, and xanthan in this order. Add softened butter and yeast.

3   Place back the bread bucket in your bread machine and close the lid. Select BASIC and then select medium darkness on CRUST COLOR. Press the START button and wait until the bread cooks.

4   Cool bread on a cooling rack before slicing.

5   Serve with grilled chicken or any of your favorite grilled meat. Note that nutrition info is only for the bread.

Nutrition: Calories: 96 Calories from fat: 36 Total Fat: 4 g Total Carbohydrates: 5 g Net Carbohydrates: 3 g

Protein: 8 g

27. Basic Sweet Yeast Bread

Preparation Time: 3 hours

Cooking Time: 0 minutes

Servings: 8

Ingredients:

- 1 egg

- ¼ cup butter

- 1/3 cup sugar

- 1 cup milk

- ½ teaspoon salt

- 2 cups almond flour

- 1 tablespoon active dry yeast

After beeping:

- fruits/ground nuts

Directions:

1   Put all of the ingredients in your bread machine, carefully following the instructions of the manufacturer (except fruits/ground nuts).

2   Set the program of your bread machine to BASIC/SWEET and set crust type to LIGHT or MEDIUM.

3   Press START.

4   Once the machine beeps, add fruits/ground nuts.

5   Wait until the cycle completes.

6   Once the loaf is ready, take the bucket out and let the loaf cool for 5 minutes.

7   Gently shake the bucket to remove the loaf.

8   Move it to a cooling rack, slice, and serve.

9   Enjoy!

Nutrition: Carbohydrates 2.7 g Fats 7.6 g Protein 8.8 g Calories 338

28. Apricot Prune Bread

Preparation Time: 3 hours

Cooking Time: 0 minutes

Servings: 8

Ingredients:

- 1 egg

- 4/5 cup whole milk

- ¼ cup apricot juice

- ¼ cup butter

- 1/5 cup sugar

- 3 cups almond flour

- 1 tablespoon instant yeast

- ¼ teaspoon salt

- 5/8 cup prunes, chopped

- 5/8 cup dried apricots, chopped

Directions:

1   Put all of the ingredients in your bread machine, carefully following the instructions of the manufacturer (except apricots and prunes).

2   Set the program of your bread machine to BASIC/SWEET and set crust type to LIGHT or MEDIUM.

3   Press START.

4   Once the machine beeps, add apricots and prunes.

5   Wait until the cycle completes.

6   Once the loaf is ready, take the bucket out and let the loaf cool for
     5 minutes.

7   Gently shake the bucket to remove the loaf.

8   Move it to a cooling rack, slice, and serve.

9   Enjoy!

Nutrition: Carbohydrates 4 g Fats 8.2 g Protein 9 g Calories 364

29. Gluten Free Chocolate Zucchini Bread

Preparation Time: 5 minutes

Cooking Time: 0 minutes

Servings: 12

Ingredients:

- 1 ½ cups coconut flour

- ¼ cup unsweetened cocoa powder

- ½ cup erythritol

- ½ tsp cinnamon

- 1 tsp baking soda

- 1 tsp baking powder

- ¼ tsp salt

- ¼ cup coconut oil, melted

- 2 eggs

- 1 tsp vanilla

- 1 cups zucchini, shredded

Directions:

1   Strip the zucchini and use paper towels to drain excess water, set aside.

2   Lightly beat eggs with coconut oil, then add to bread machine pan.

3   Add the remaining ingredients to the pan.

4   Set bread machine to gluten free.

5   When the bread is done, remove the bread machine pan from the bread machine.

6   Cool to some extent before transferring to a cooling rack.

7   You can store your bread for up to 5 days.

Nutrition: Calories 185 Carbohydrates 6 g Fats 17 g Protein 5 g

30. Not Your Everyday Bread

Preparation Time: 7 minutes

Cooking Time: 0 minutes

Servings: 12

Ingredients:

- 1 tsp active dry yeast
- 1 tbsp. inulin
- ½ cup warm water
- ¾ cup almond flour
- ¼ cup golden flaxseed, ground
- 1 tbsp. whey protein isolate
- 1 tbsp. psyllium husk finely ground
- 1tsp xanthan gum
- 1 tsp baking powder
- 1 tsp salt
- ¼ tsp cream of tartar
- ¼ tsp ginger, ground
- 1 egg
- egg whites
- 1 tbsp. ghee

- 1 tbsp. apple cider vinegar

- ¼ cup sour cream

Directions:

1 Pour wet ingredients into bread machine pan.

2 Add dry ingredients with the yeast on top.

3 Set bread machine to basic bread setting.

4 When the bread is done, remove the bread machine pan from the bread machine.

5 Cool to some extent before transferring to a cooling rack.

6 You can store your bread for up to 5 days.

Nutrition: Calories 175 Carbohydrates 6 g Fats 14 g Protein 5 g

NUT AND SEED BREADS

31.Flax and Sunflower Seed Bread

Preparation Time: 5 Minutes

Cooking Time: 25 Minutes

Servings: 8

Ingredients:

- 1 1/3 cups water

- 2 tablespoons butter softened

- 3 tablespoons honey

- 2/3 cups of bread flour

- 1 teaspoon salt

- 1 teaspoon active dry yeast

- 1/2 cup flax seeds

- 1/2 cup sunflower seeds

Directions:

1. With the manufacturer's suggested order, add all the ingredients (apart from sunflower seeds) to the bread machine's pan.

2. The select basic white cycle, then press start.

3. Just in the knead cycle that your machine signals alert sounds, add the sunflower seeds.

Nutrition: Calories: 140 calories; Sodium: 169 Total Carbohydrate: 22.7 Cholesterol: 4 Protein: 4.2 Total Fat: 4.2

32.   Honey and Flaxseed Bread

Preparation Time: 5 Minutes

Cooking Time: 25 Minutes

Servings: 8

Ingredients:

- 1 1/8 cups water

- 1 1/2 tablespoons flaxseed oil

- 3 tablespoons honey

- 1/2 tablespoon liquid lecithin

- 3 cups whole wheat flour

- 1/2 cup flax seed

- 2 tablespoons bread flour

- 3 tablespoons whey powder

- 1 1/2 teaspoons sea salt

- 2 teaspoons active dry yeast

Directions:

1   In the bread machine pan, put in all of the ingredients following the order recommended by the manufacturer.

2   Choose the Wheat cycle on the machine and press the Start button to run the machine.

Nutrition: Calories: 174 calories; Protein: 7.1 Total Fat: 4.9 Sodium: 242 Total Carbohydrate: 30.8 Cholesterol: 1

33. Pumpkin and Sunflower Seed Bread

Preparation Time: 5 Minutes

Cooking Time: 25 Minutes

Servings: 8

Ingredients:

- 1 (.25 ounce) package instant yeast
- 1 cup of warm water
- 1/4 cup honey
- 4 teaspoons vegetable oil
- 3 cups whole wheat flour
- 1/4 cup wheat bran (optional)
- 1 teaspoon salt
- 1/3 cup sunflower seeds
- 1/3 cup shelled, toasted, chopped pumpkin seeds

Directions:

1   Into the bread machine, put the ingredients according to the order suggested by the manufacturer.

2   Next is setting the machine to the whole wheat setting, then press the start button.

3   You can add the pumpkin and sunflower seeds at the beep if your bread machine has a signal for nuts or fruit.

Nutrition: Calories: 148 calories; Total Carbohydrate: 24.1 Cholesterol: 0 Protein: 5.1 Total Fat: 4.8 Sodium: 158

34.   Seven Grain Bread

Preparation Time: 5 Minutes

Cooking Time: 25 Minutes

Servings: 8

Ingredients:

- 1 1/3 cups warm water

- 1 tablespoon active dry yeast

- 3 tablespoons dry milk powder

- 2 tablespoons vegetable oil

- 2 tablespoons honey

- 2 teaspoons salt

- 1 egg

- 1 cup whole wheat flour

- 1/2 cups bread flour

- 3/4 cup 7-grain cereal

Directions:

1   Follow the order of putting the ingredients into the pan of the bread machine recommended by the manufacturer.

2   Choose the Whole Wheat Bread cycle on the machine and press the Start button to run the machine.

Nutrition: Calories: 285 calories; Total Fat: 5.2 Sodium: 629 Total Carbohydrate: 50.6 Cholesterol: 24; Protein: 9.8

35.   Wheat Bread with Flax Seed

Preparation Time: 5 Minutes

Cooking Time: 25 Minutes

Servings: 8

Ingredients:

- 1 (.25 ounce) package active dry yeast

- 1 1/4 cups whole wheat flour

- 3/4 cup ground flax seed

- 1 cup bread flour

- 1 tablespoon vital wheat gluten

- 2 tablespoons dry milk powder

- 1 teaspoon salt

- 1 1/2 tablespoons vegetable oil

- 1/4 cup honey

- 1 1/2 cups water

Directions:

1   In the bread machine pan, put the ingredients following the order recommendation of the manufacturer.

2   Make sure to select the cycle and then press Start.

Nutrition: Calories: 168 calories Total Carbohydrate: 22.5 Cholesterol: 1

Protein: 5.5 Total Fat: 7.3 Sodium: 245

36. High Fiber Bread

Preparation Time: 5 Minutes

Cooking Time: 25 Minutes

Servings: 8

Ingredients:

- 1 2/3 cups warm water

- 4 teaspoons molasses

- 1 tablespoon active dry yeast

- 2/3 cups whole wheat flour

- 3/4 cup ground flax seed

- 2/3 cup bread flour

- 1/2 cup oat bran

- 1/3 cup rolled oats

- 1/3 cup amaranth seeds

- 1 teaspoon salt

Directions:

1   In the bread machine pan, put in the water, molasses, yeast, wheat flour, ground flaxseed, bread flour, oat bran, rolled oats, amaranth seeds, and salt in the manufacturer's suggested order of

ingredients. Choose the Dough cycle on the machine and press the Start button; let the machine finish the whole Dough cycle.

2   Put the dough on a clean surface that is covered with a little bit of flour. Shape the dough into two loaves and put it on a baking stone. Use a slightly wet cloth to shelter the loaves and allow it to rise in volume for about 1 hour until it has doubled in size.

3   Preheat the bread machine to 375°F.

4   Put in the warm-up bread machine and bake for 20-25 minutes until the top part of the loaf turns golden brown. Let the loaf slide onto a clean working surface and tap the loaf's bottom part gently. The bread is done if you hear a hollow sound when tapped.

Nutrition: Calories: 101 calories; Total Fat: 2.1 Sodium: 100 Total Carbohydrate: 18.2 Cholesterol: 0 Protein: 4

37. High Flavor Bran Head

Preparation Time: 5 Minutes

Cooking Time: 25 Minutes

Servings: 8

Ingredients:

- 1 1/2 cups warm water
- 2 tablespoons dry milk powder
- 2 tablespoons vegetable oil
- 2 tablespoons molasses
- 2 tablespoons honey
- 1 1/2 teaspoons salt
- 1/4 cups whole wheat flour
- 1 1/4 cups bread flour
- 1 cup whole bran cereal
- 2 teaspoons active dry yeast

Directions:

1   In the pan of your bread machine, move all the ingredients directed by the machine's maker.

2   Set the machine to either the whole grain or whole wheat setting.

Nutrition: Calories: 146 calories Total Fat: 2.4 Sodium: 254 Total Carbohydrate: 27.9 Cholesterol: 1 Protein: 4.6

38.   High Protein Bread

Preparation Time: 5 Minutes

Cooking Time: 25 Minutes

Servings: 8

Ingredients:

- 2 teaspoons active dry yeast

- 1 cup bread flour

- 1 cup whole wheat flour

- 1/4 cup soy flour

- 1/4 cup powdered soy milk

- 1/4 cup oat bran

- 1 tablespoon canola oil

- 1 tablespoon honey

- 1 teaspoon salt

- 1 cup of water

Directions:

1   Into the bread machine's pan, put the ingredients by following the order suggested by the manufacturer.

2   Set the machine to either the regular setting or the basic medium.

3   Push the Start button.

Nutrition: Calories: 137 calories Total Fat: 2.4 Sodium: 235 Total Carbohydrate: 24.1 Cholesterol: 0 Protein: 6.5

39.   Whole Wheat Bread with Sesame Seeds

Preparation Time: 5 Minutes

Cooking Time: 25 Minutes

Servings: 8

Ingredients:

- 1/2 cup water
- 2 teaspoons honey
- 1 tablespoon vegetable oil
- 3/4 cup grated zucchini
- 3/4 cup whole wheat flour
- 3 cups bread flour
- 1 tablespoon chopped fresh basil
- 2 teaspoons sesame seeds
- 1 teaspoon salt
- 1 1/2 teaspoons active dry yeast

Directions:

1   Follow the order of putting the ingredients into the bread machine pan recommended by the manufacturer.

2   Choose the Basic Bread cycle or the Normal setting on the machine.

Nutrition: Calories: 153 calories Sodium: 235 Total Carbohydrate: 28.3 Cholesterol: 0 Protein: 5 Total Fat: 2.3

40.   Bagels with Poppy Seeds

Preparation Time: 5 Minutes

Cooking Time: 25 Minutes

Servings: 8

Ingredients:

- 1 cup of warm water

- 1 1/2 teaspoons salt

- 2 tablespoons white sugar

- 3 cups bread flour

- 1/4 teaspoons active dry yeast

- 4 quarts boiling water

- 3 tablespoons white sugar

- 1 tablespoon cornmeal

- 1 egg white

- 3 tablespoons poppy seeds

Directions:

1   In the bread machine's pan, pour in the water, salt, sugar, flour, and yeast following the order of ingredients suggested by the manufacturer. Choose the Dough setting on the machine.

2   Once the machine has finished the whole cycle, place the dough on a clean surface covered with a little bit of flour; let it rest. While the dough is resting on the floured surface, put 3 quarts of water in a big pot and let it boil. Add in 3 tablespoons of sugar and mix.

3   Divide the dough evenly into nine portions and shape each into a small ball. Press down each dough ball until it is flat. Use your thumb to make a shack in the center of each flattened dough. Increase the whole's size in the center and smoothen out the dough around the whole area by spinning the dough on your thumb or finger. Use a clean cloth to cover the formed bagels and let them sit for 10 minutes.

4   Cover the bottom part of an ungreased baking sheet evenly with cornmeal. Place the bagels gently into the boiling water. Let it boil for 1 minute and flip it on the other side halfway through. Let the bagels drain quickly on a clean towel. Place the boiled bagels onto the prepared baking sheet. Coat the topmost of each bagel with egg white and top it off with your preferred toppings.

5   Put the bagels into the preheated 375°F (190°C) bread machine and bake for 20-25 minutes until it turns nice brown.

Nutrition: Calories: 50 calories Total Fat: 1.3 Sodium: 404 Total Carbohydrate: 8.8 Cholesterol: 0 Protein: 1.4

41.Bruce's Honey Sesame Bread

Preparation Time: 5 Minutes

Cooking Time: 25 Minutes

Servings: 8

Ingredients:

- 1 1/4 cups water

- 1/4 cup honey

- 1 tablespoon powdered buttermilk

- 1 1/2 teaspoons salt

- 3 cups bread flour

- 3 tablespoons wheat bran

- 1/2 cup sesame seeds, toasted

- 1/4 teaspoons active dry yeast

Directions:

1 Into the bread machine's pan, place all the ingredients by following the order endorsed by your machine's manufacturer.

2 Set the mechanism to the Basic Bread cycle.

Nutrition: Calories: 62 calories Total Carbohydrate: 8.4 Cholesterol: 1 Protein: 1.7 Total Fat: 3.1 Sodium: 295

42. Moroccan Ksra

Preparation Time: 5 Minutes

Cooking Time: 25 Minutes

Servings: 8

Ingredients:

- 7/8 cup water

- 1/4 cups bread flour

- 3/4 cup semolina flour

- 1 teaspoon anise seed

- 1 1/2 teaspoons salt

- 1/2 teaspoon white sugar

- 2 teaspoons active dry yeast

- 1 tablespoon olive oil

- 1 tablespoon sesame seed

Directions:

1 In a bread machine, put the first set of ingredients according to the manufacturer's recommendation. Set to DOUGH cycle and select Start. In this procedure, refrain from mixing in the sesame seeds and olive oil.

2   When the dough cycle signal stops, take the dough from the machine and deflate by punching it down. Cut the dough into two halves and form it into balls. Pat the balls into a 3/4-inch thickness. Put the flattened dough on a floured baking sheet. Cover the baking sheet with towels and let it stand for about 30 minutes to rise to double.

3   Set the bread machine to 200 degrees C (400 degrees F) to preheat. Spread the top of the loaves with olive oil using a brush and garnish with sesame seeds, if preferred. Using a fork, puncture the top of each loaf all over.

4   Place the pans in the heated bread machine, then bake for 20 to 25 minutes, or until colors are golden and they sound hollow when tapped. Serve either warm or cold.

Nutrition: Calories: 111 calories Total Fat: 1.6 Sodium: 219 Total Carbohydrate: 20.2 Cholesterol: 0 Protein: 3.6

43. Bread Sticks with Sesame Seeds

Preparation Time: 5 Minutes

Cooking Time: 25 Minutes

Servings: 8

Ingredients:

- 1 1/3 cups warm water

- 3 tablespoons butter softened

- 3 cups bread flour

- 2 teaspoons salt

- 1/4 cup white sugar

- 1/4 cup sesame seeds

- 2 tablespoons dry milk powder

- 1/2 teaspoons active dry yeast

Directions:

1 Into the bread machine pan, set the ingredients according to the order given by the manufacturer. Put the machine to the Dough cycle and then push the Start button. Use cooking spray to spritz two baking sheets.

2 Preheat the bread machine. After the dough cycle comes to an end, place the dough onto a lightly oiled surface. Separate the dough

into 18 pieces. Fold every piece on a board oiled from the middle of the amount to the outside edges. It is to create breadsticks. Transfer the breadsticks onto the prepared pans placing at least one inch apart.

3   Bake for around 15 minutes using the bread machine until golden. Transfer to a wire rack to cool.

Nutrition: Calories: 154 Total Fat: 3.5 Sodium: 278 Total Carbohydrate: 26 Cholesterol: 5 Protein: 4.5

44.   Apricot Cake Bread

Preparation Time: 20 Minutes

Cooking Time: 4 Hours and 30 Minutes

Servings: 8

Ingredients:

- 5 cups of Water, lukewarm

- 2 Eggs, at room temperature

- 3 cups of Orange juice

- 1/3 cup of Butter, unsalted, softened

- 2 oz. Dried apricots, snipped

- 3 cups of All-purpose flour

- 1/3 cups Sugar

- 1 tbsp. Baking powder

- 1 teaspoon Baking soda

- 1 teaspoon Salt

- 3 oz. of Chopped nuts

Directions:

1   Take a medium bowl, place apricots in it, pour in water, and let soak for 30 minutes.

2   Then remove apricots from the water, reserve the water, and chop apricots into pieces.

3   Gather the remaining ingredients needed for the bread.

4   Power on bread machine that has about 2 pounds of the bread pan.

5   Put all the ingredients into the bread machine pan, except for apricots and nuts, in the order mentioned in the ingredients list.

6   Press the "Bread" button, press the start button, let mixture knead for 5 minutes, add chopped apricots and nuts and continue kneading for 5 minutes until all the pieces have thoroughly combined and incorporated.

7   Select the "basic/white" cycle, press the up/down arrow to do baking for 4 hours, choose light or medium color for the crust, and press the start button.

8   When the timer of the bread machine beeps, open the machine.

9   It should come out spotless, else bake for another 10 to 15 minutes.

10   Cut bread into eight slices and then serve.

Nutrition: Calories: 144 Fat (g): 3.6 Protein (g): 3.9 Carbs: 25.6

45.   Cherry and Almond Bread

Preparation Time: 10 Minutes

Cooking Time: 4 Hours

Servings: 8

Ingredients:

- 3 cups of Milk, lukewarm

- 2 cups of Butter, unsalted, softened

- 1 Egg, at room temperature

- 3 cups Bread flour

- 1 oz. Dried cherries

- 2 oz. Slivered almonds, toasted

- 1 teaspoon of Salt

- 1 teaspoon of Dry yeast, active

- ½ cup of Sugar

Directions:

1   Gather all the ingredients needed for the bread.

2   Power on bread machine that has about 2 pounds of the bread pan.

3   Add all the ingredients in the order mentioned in the ingredients list into the bread machine pan.

4   Press the "Dough" button, key the left button, and let the mixture knead for 5 to 10 minutes.

5   Then select the "basic/white" down arrow to set baking time to 4 hours, select light or medium color for the crust, and press the start button.

6   Then prudently lift out the bread and put it on a wire rack for 1 hour or more until cooled.

7   Cut bread into sixteen slices and then serve.

Nutrition: Calories: 125 Fat (g): 3 Protein (g): 4 Carbs: 20.4

46. Nutty Wheat Bread

Preparation Time: 10 Minutes

Cooking Time: 4 Hours

Servings: 12

Ingredients:

- 3 cups of Water, lukewarm
- 1 teaspoon of Olive oil
- 1 teaspoon of Honey
- 3 oz. Molasses
- 3 cups of Whole wheat flour
- 1 cup Bread flour
- 1 teaspoon Dry yeast, active
- 1 teaspoon Salt
- 1 oz. Chopped pecans
- 1 oz. Chopped walnuts

Directions:

1. Gather all the ingredients needed for the bread.

2. Power on bread machine that has about 2 pounds of the bread pan.

3. Add all the ingredients in the order listed in the ingredients list into the bread machine pan except for pecans and nuts.

4   Press the "Dough" switch, press the start button, let the mixture knead for 5 minutes, add pecans and nuts, and then continue kneading for another 5 minutes until all the ingredients have thoroughly combined and incorporated.

5   Then select the "basic/white" cycle, press the up/down arrow to make the baking time to 4 hours.

6   Select light or medium color for the crust and press the start button.

7   Then put the bread on a wire rack for 1 hour or more until cooled.

8   Cut bread into twelve slices and then serve.

Nutrition: Calories: 187 Fat (g): 7 Protein (g): 5 Carbs: 28

47.   Hazelnut Yeast Bread

Preparation Time: 10 Minutes

Cooking Time: 3 Hours

Servings: 16

Ingredients:

- 2cups of Milk, lukewarm

- ½ cup of Butter, unsalted, melted

- 3 Egg, at room temperature

- 1 oz. Almond extract, unsweetened

- 1 teaspoon of Salt

- 3 cups Bread flour

- ½ cups Sugar

- 1 teaspoon of Dry yeast, active

- 1 oz. Chopped hazelnuts, toasted

Directions:

1   Gather all the ingredients needed for the bread.

2   Then power on bread machine that has about 2 pounds of the bread pan.

3   Add all the ingredients in the order stated in the ingredients list into the bread machine pan except for nuts.

4   Press the "Dough" button, press the start button, let the mixture knead for 5 minutes, add nuts, and then knead for another 5 minutes until all the ingredients have thoroughly combined and incorporated.

5   Then select the "basic/white" cycle, or press the up/down arrow to set baking time to 3 hours.

6   Select light or medium color for the crust and then press the start button.

7   Put it on a wire rack for 1 hour or more until cooled.

8   Cut bread into sixteen slices and then serve.

Nutrition: Calories: 139 Fat (g): 6 Protein (g): 5 Carbs: 18

48.   Date-Nut Yeast Bread

Preparation Time: 10 Minutes

Cooking Time: 4 Hours

Servings: 12

Ingredients:

- 3 cups of Water, lukewarm

- ¼ cup of Butter, unsalted, softened

- 3 cups of Bread flour

- 1 teaspoon of Dry yeast, active

- 1 cup of Brown sugar

- 1 teaspoon of Salt

- 1 0z. Dates, chopped

- 1 Oz. Walnuts, chopped

Directions:

1   Gather all the ingredients needed for the bread.

2   Power on bread machine that has about 2 pounds of the bread pan.

3   Add all the ingredients in the order cited in the ingredients list into the bread machine pan.

4   Press the "Dough" button, push the start button.

5   Allow the mixture to knead for 5 to 10 minutes until all the pieces have been thoroughly combined and incorporated.

6   Select the "basic/white" cycle, or press the up/down arrow to set baking day to 4 hours.

7   Select light or medium color for the crust and then press the start button.

8   Then handover it to a wire rack for one hour or more until cooled.

9   Cut bread into twelve slices and then serve.

Nutrition: Calories: 123 Fat (g): 2 Protein (g): 4 Carbs: 24

49.   Walnut Bread with Dry Yeast

Preparation Time: 10 Minutes

Cooking Time: 4 Hours

Servings: 12

Ingredients:

- 3 cups of Water, lukewarm

- 2 Egg, at room temperature

- ½ cup Butter, unsalted, softened

- 3 cups of Bread flour

- 1 teaspoon Dry yeast, active

- 3 tbsp. of Dry milk powder, nonfat

- 1/3 cups Sugar

- 1 teaspoon of Salt

- 1oz. of Chopped walnuts, toasted

Directions:

1   Gather all the ingredients needed for the bread.

2   Then power on bread machine that has about 2 pounds of the bread pan.

3   Add all the ingredients in the order revealed in the ingredients list into the bread machine pan.

4   Press the "Dough" button, press the start button, and let the mixture knead for 5 to 10 minutes until all the ingredients have thoroughly combined and incorporated.

5   Select the "basic/white" cycle, key the up/down arrow to set baking time to 4 hours.

6   Select light or medium color for the crust and press the start button.

7   Then sensibly lift out the bread and put it on a wire rack for 1 hour or more until cooled.

8   Cut bread into twelve slices and then serve.

Nutrition: Calories: 135 Fat (g): 5 Protein (g): 5 Carbs: 19

50.   Cranberry Walnut Bread

Preparation Time: 10 Minutes

Cooking Time: 4 Hours

Servings: 16

Ingredients:

- 3 cups of Water, lukewarm

- ½ cup of Butter, unsalted, softened

- 3 cups of Bread flour

- 1 teaspoon of Dry yeast, active

- 2 tbsp. Brown sugar

- 1 teaspoon of Salt

- 1 oz. Ground cinnamon

- 1 oz. Chopped walnuts

- 1 oz. Dried cranberries

Directions:

1   Gather all the ingredients needed for the bread.

2   Power on bread machine that has about 2 pounds of the bread pan.

3   Add all the ingredients except for nuts and cranberries into the bread machine pan in the order mentioned in the ingredients list.

4   Press the "Dough" button, press the start button, let the mixture knead for 5 minutes, then add walnuts and cranberries and continue kneading for 5 minutes until all the ingredients have thoroughly combined and incorporated.

5   Select the "basic/white" cycle, press the up/down arrow to set baking time to 4 hours.

6   Select light or medium color for the crust and press the start button.

7   Then carefully lift the bread and transfer it to a wire rack for 1 hour or additional until cooled.

8   Cut bread into slices and then serve.

Nutrition: Calories: 134 Fat (g): 3 Protein (g): 4 Carbs: 24

51.Pumpkin Bread with Walnuts

Preparation Time: 10 Minutes

Cooking Time: 1 Hour

Servings: 16

Ingredients:

- 1 tbsp. Olive oil

- 2 oz. Pumpkin puree

- 2 Eggs, at room temperature

- 3 cups of All-purpose flour

- 1 teaspoon Baking powder

- 1 teaspoon Baking soda

- 1 oz. Ground ginger

- 1/3 cups of Sugar

- 1 teaspoon of Salt

- 1 oz. Ground cinnamon

- 1 oz. Ground nutmeg

- 1 oz. Chopped walnuts

Directions:

1   Gather all the ingredients needed for the bread.

2   Power on bread machine that has about 2 pounds of the bread pan.

3   Take a large mixing bowl, add eggs to it and then beat in sugar, oil, and pumpkin puree using an electric mixer until smooth and well blended.

4   Beat in salt, all the spices, baking powder, and soda, and then beat in flour, ½-cup at a time, until incorporated.

5   Pour the batter into the bread pan, top with nuts, select the "cake/quick bread" cycle, or press the up/down arrow to set the baking time to 1 hour.

6   Choose light or medium color for the crust and then press the start button.

7   Then carefully get out the bread and hand it to a wire rack for 1 hour or more until cooled.

8   Cut bread into sixteen slices and then serve.

Nutrition: Calories: 166 Fat (g): 9 Protein (g): 3 Carbs: 19

CONCLUSION

This book has presented you to some of the easiest and delicious bread recipes you can find. One of the most mutual struggles for anyone following the diet is that they have to cut out so many of the foods they love, like sugary foods and starchy bread products. This book helps you overcome both those issues.

Focus your mindset toward the positive. Through a diet, you can help prevent diabetes, heart diseases, and respiratory problems. If you already feel pain from any of these, a diet under a doctor's supervision can greatly improve your condition.

These loaves of bread are made using the normal Ingredients you can find locally, so there's no need to have to order anything or have to go to any specialty stores for any of them. With these pieces of bread, you can enjoy the same meals you used to enjoy but stay on track with your diet as much as you want.

Lose the weight you want to lose, feel great, and still get to indulge in that piping hot piece of bread now and then. Spread on your favorite topping, and your bread craving will be satisfied.

Moreover, we have learned that the bread machine is a vital tool to have in our kitchen. It is not that hard to put into use. All you need to learn is how it functions and what its features are. You also need to use it more often to learn the dos and don'ts of using the machine.

The bread machine comes with a set of instructions that you must learn from the manual to use it the right way. There is a certain way of loading the Ingredients that must be followed, and the instructions vary according to the make and the model. So, when you first get a machine, sit down and learn the manual from start to finish; this allows you to put it to good use and get better results. The manual will tell you exactly what to put in it, as well as the correct settings to use, according to the different ingredients and the type of bread you want to make.

Having a bread machine in your kitchen makes life easy. Whether you are a professional baker or a home cook, this appliance will help you get the best bread texture and flavors with minimum effort. Bread making is an art, and it takes extra care and special technique to deal with a specific type of flour and bread machine that enables you to do so even when you are not a professional. In this book, we have discussed all bread machines and how we can put them to good use. Basic information about flour and yeast is also discussed to give all the beginners an idea of how to deal with the major ingredients of bread and what variety to use to get a particular type of bread. And finally, some delicious bread recipes were shared so that you can try them at home!

CPSIA information can be obtained
at www.ICGtesting.com
Printed in the USA
BVHW091056030521
606332BV00004B/496